Prayer

D1452516

Ellen G. White

Kessinger Publishing's Rare Reprints

Thousands of Scarce and Hard-to-Find Books on These and other Subjects!

- Americana
- Ancient Mysteries
- Animals
- Anthropology
- Architecture
- Arts
- Astrology
- Bibliographies
- Biographies & Memoirs
- Body, Mind & Spirit
- Business & Investing
- Children & Young Adult
- Collectibles
- Comparative Religions
- Crafts & Hobbies
- Earth Sciences
- Education
- Ephemera
- Fiction
- Folklore
- Geography
- Health & Diet
- History
- Hobbies & Leisure
- Humor
- Illustrated Books
- Language & Culture
- Law
- Life Sciences

- Literature
- Medicine & Pharmacy
- Metaphysical
- Music
- Mystery & Crime
- Mythology
- Natural History
- Outdoor & Nature
- Philosophy
- Poetry
- Political Science
- Science
- Psychiatry & Psychology
- Reference
- Religion & Spiritualism
- Rhetoric
- Sacred Books
- Science Fiction
- Science & Technology
- Self-Help
- Social Sciences
- Symbolism
- Theatre & Drama
- Theology
- Travel & Explorations
- War & Military
- Women
- Yoga
- *Plus Much More!*

We kindly invite you to view our catalog list at:
http://www.kessinger.net

Because this article has been extracted from a parent book, it may have non-pertinent text at the beginning or end of it.

Any blank pages following the article are necessary for our book production requirements. The article herein is complete.

PRAYER

"Ask, and it shall be given you"

Matt. 7·7

'Lend me three loaves; for a
friend of mine in his journey
is come to me, and I have
nothing to set before him.

ASKING TO GIVE

Asking to Give

*C*HRIST was continually receiving from the Father that He might communicate to us. "The word which ye hear," He said, "is not Mine, but the Father's which sent Me." "The Son of man came not to be ministered unto, but to minister."[1] Not for Himself, but for others, He lived and thought and prayed. From hours spent with God He came forth morning by morning, to bring the light of heaven to men. Daily He received a fresh baptism of the Holy Spirit. In the early hours of the new day the Lord awakened Him from His slumbers, and His soul and His lips were anointed with grace, that He might impart to others. His words were given Him fresh from the heavenly courts, words that He might speak in season to the weary and oppressed. "The Lord God hath given Me," He said, "the tongue of the learned, that I should know how to speak a word in season to him that is weary: He wakeneth morning by morning, He wakeneth Mine ear to hear as the learned."[2]

Based on Luke 11:1-13   [1]John 14:24; Matt. 20:28   [2]Isa. 50:4   (139)

Christ's disciples were much impressed by His prayers and by His habit of communion with God. One day after a short absence from their Lord, they found Him absorbed in supplication. Seeming unconscious of their presence, He continued praying aloud. The hearts of the disciples were deeply moved. As He ceased praying, they exclaimed, "Lord, teach us to pray."

In answer, Christ repeated the Lord's prayer, as He had given it in the sermon on the mount. Then in a parable He illustrated the lesson He desired to teach them.

"Which of you," He said, "shall have a friend, and shall go unto him at midnight, and say unto him, Friend, lend me three loaves; for a friend of mine in his journey is come to me, and I have nothing to set before him? And he from within shall answer and say, Trouble me not; the door is now shut, and my children are with me in bed: I can not rise and give thee. I say unto you, Though he will not rise and give him because he is his friend, yet because of his importunity he will rise and give him as many as he needeth."

Here Christ represents the petitioner as asking that he may give again. He must obtain the bread, else he can not supply the necessities of a weary, belated wayfarer. Though his neighbor is unwilling to be troubled, he will not desist his pleading; his friend must be relieved; and at last his importunity is rewarded; his wants are supplied.

In like manner the disciples were to seek blessings from God. In the feeding of the multitude and in the sermon on the bread from heaven, Christ had opened to them their work as His representatives. They were to give the bread of life to the people. He who had appointed their work, saw how often their faith would be tried. Often they would be thrown into unexpected positions, and would realize their human insufficiency. Souls that were hungering for the bread of life would come to them, and they would feel themselves to be destitute and helpless. They must receive spiritual food, or they would have nothing to impart. But they were not to turn one soul away unfed. Christ directs them to the source of supply. The man whose friend came to him for entertainment, even at the unseasonable hour of midnight, did not turn him away. He had nothing to set before him, but he went to one who had food, and pressed his request, until the neighbor supplied his need. And would not God, who had sent His servants to feed the hungry, supply their need for His own work?

But the selfish neighbor in the parable does not represent the character of God. The lesson is drawn, not by comparison, but by contrast. A selfish man will grant an urgent request, in order to rid himself of one who disturbs his rest. But God delights to give. He is full of compassion, and He longs to grant the requests of those who come unto Him in faith. He gives to us that we may minister to others, and thus become like Himself.

Christ declares, "Ask, and it shall be given you; seek, and ye shall find; knock, and it shall be opened unto you. For every one that asketh receiveth; and he that seeketh findeth; and to him that knocketh it shall be opened."

The Saviour continues: "If a son shall ask bread of any of you that is a father, will he give him a stone? or if he ask a fish, will he for a fish give him a serpent? or if he shall ask an egg, will he offer him a scorpion? If ye then, being evil, know how to give good gifts unto your children, how much more shall your Heavenly Father give the Holy Spirit to them that ask Him?"

In order to strengthen our confidence in God, Christ teaches us to address Him by a new name, a name entwined with the dearest associations of the human heart. He gives us the privilege of calling the infinite God our Father. This name, spoken to Him and of Him, is a sign of our love and trust toward Him, and a pledge of His regard and relationship to us. Spoken when asking His favor or blessing, it is as music in His ears. That we might not think it presumption to call Him by this name, He has repeated it again and again. He desires us to become familiar with the appellation.

God regards us as His children. He has redeemed us out of the careless world, and has chosen us to become members of the royal family, sons and daughters of the heavenly King. He invites us to trust in Him with a trust deeper and stronger than that of a child in his earthly father. Parents love their children, but the love of God is larger, broader, deeper than human love can possibly be. It is immeasurable. Then if earthly parents know how to give good gifts to their children, how much more shall our Father in heaven give the Holy Spirit to those who ask Him?

Christ's lessons in regard to prayer should be carefully considered. There is a divine science in prayer, and His illustration brings to view principles that all need to understand. He shows what is the true spirit of prayer, He teaches the necessity of perseverance in presenting our requests to God, and assures us of His willingness to hear and answer prayer.

Our prayers are not to be a selfish asking, merely for our own benefit. We are to ask that we may give. The principle of Christ's life must be the principle of our lives. "For their sakes," He said, speaking of His disciples, "I sanctify Myself, that they also might be sanctified."[1] The same devotion, the same self-sacrifice, the same subjection to the claims of the word of God, that were manifest in Christ, must be seen in His servants. Our mission to the world is not to serve or please ourselves; we are to glorify

[1] John 17 : 19

God by co-operating with Him to save sinners. We are to ask blessings from God that we may communicate to others. The capacity for receiving is preserved only by imparting. We can not continue to receive heavenly treasure without communicating to those around us.

In the parable the petitioner was again and again repulsed, but he did not relinquish his purpose. So our prayers do not always seem to receive an immediate answer; but Christ teaches that we should not cease to pray. Prayer is not to work any change in God; it is to bring us into harmony with God. When we make request of Him, He may see that it is necessary for us to search our hearts and repent of sin. Therefore He takes us through test and trial, He brings us through humiliation, that we may see what hinders the working of His Holy Spirit through us.

There are conditions to the fulfilment of God's promises, and prayer can never take the place of duty. "If ye love Me," Christ says, "keep My commandments." "He that hath My commandments, and keepeth them, he it is that loveth Me; and he that loveth Me shall be loved of My Father, and I will love him, and will manifest Myself to him."[1] Those who bring their petitions to God, claiming His promise while they do not comply with the conditions, insult Jehovah. They bring the name of Christ as their authority for the fulfilment of the promise, but they do not those things that would show faith in Christ and love for Him.

Many are forfeiting the condition of acceptance with the Father. We need to examine closely the deed of trust wherewith we approach God. If we are disobedient, we bring to the Lord a note to be cashed when we have not fulfilled the conditions that would make it payable to us. We present to God His promises, and ask Him to fulfil them, when by so doing He would dishonor His own name.

[1] John 14 : 15, 21

The promise is, "If ye abide in Me, and My words abide in you, ye shall ask what ye will, and it shall be done unto you."[1] And John declares: "Hereby we do know that we know Him, if we keep His commandments. He that saith, I know Him, and keepeth not His commandments, is a liar, and the truth is not in him. But whoso keepeth His word, in him verily is the love of God perfected."

One of Christ's last commands to His disciples was, "Love one another as I have loved you."[3] Do we obey this command, or are we indulging sharp, unchristlike traits of character? If we have in any way grieved or wounded others, it is our duty to confess our fault, and seek for reconciliation. This is an essential preparation that we may come before God in faith, to ask His blessing.

There is another matter too often neglected by those who seek the Lord in prayer. Have you been honest with God? By the prophet Malachi the Lord declares, "Even from the days of your fathers ye are gone away from Mine ordinances, and have not kept them. Return unto Me, and I will return unto you, saith the Lord of hosts. But ye said, Wherein shall we return? Will a man rob God? Yet ye have robbed Me. But ye say, Wherein have we robbed Thee? In tithes and offerings."[4]

As the Giver of every blessing, God claims a certain portion of all we possess. This is His provision to sustain the preaching of the gospel. And by making this return to God, we are to show our appreciation of His gifts. But if we withhold from Him that which is His own, how can we claim His blessing? If we are unfaithful stewards of earthly things, how can we expect Him to entrust us with the things of heaven? It may be that here is the secret of unanswered prayer.

But the Lord in His great mercy is ready to forgive, and He says, "Bring ye all the tithes into the storehouse,

[1] John 15:7   [2] 1 John 2:3-5   [3] John 13:34   [4] Mal. 3:7, 8

that there may be meat in Mine house, and prove Me now herewith, . . . if I will not open you the windows of heaven, and pour you out a blessing, that there shall not be room enough to receive it. And I will rebuke the devourer for your sakes, and he shall not destroy the fruits of your ground; neither shall your vine cast her fruit before the time in the field. . . . And all nations shall call you blessed; for ye shall be a delightsome land, saith the Lord of hosts."[1]

So it is with every other one of God's requirements. All His gifts are promised on condition of obedience. God has a heaven full of blessings for those who will co-operate with Him. All who obey Him may with confidence claim the fulfilment of His promises.

But we must show a firm, undeviating trust in God. Often He delays to answer us, in order to try our faith or test the genuineness of our desire. Having asked according to His word, we should believe His promise, and press our petitions with a determination that will not be denied.

God does not say, Ask once, and you shall receive. He bids us ask. Unwearyingly persist in prayer. The persistent asking brings the petitioner into a more earnest attitude, and gives him an increased desire to receive the things for which he asks. Christ said to Martha at the grave of Lazarus, "If thou wouldst believe, thou shouldst see the glory of God."[2]

But many have not a living faith. This is why they do not see more of the power of God. Their weakness is the result of their unbelief. They have more faith in their own working than in the working of God for them. They take themselves into their own keeping. They plan and devise, but pray little, and have little real trust in God. They think they have faith, but it is only the impulse of the moment. Failing to realize their own need, or God's

10   [1] Mal. 3 : 10-12   [2] John 11 : 40

willingness to give, they do not persevere in keeping their requests before the Lord.

Our prayers are to be as earnest and persistent as was the petition of the needy friend who asked for the loaves at midnight. The more earnestly and steadfastly we ask, the closer will be our spiritual union with Christ. We shall receive increased blessings because we have increased faith.

Our part is to pray and believe. Watch unto prayer. Watch, and co-operate with the prayer-hearing God. Bear in mind that "we are laborers together with God."[1] Speak and act in harmony with your prayers. It will make an infinite difference with you whether trial shall prove your faith to be genuine, or show that your prayers are only a form.

When perplexities arise, and difficulties confront you, look not for help to humanity. Trust all with God. The practise of telling our difficulties to others, only makes us weak, and brings no strength to them. It lays upon them the burden of our spiritual infirmities, which they can not relieve. We seek the strength of erring, finite man, when we might have the strength of the unerring, infinite God.

You need not go to the ends of the earth for wisdom, for God is near. It is not the capabilities you now possess, or ever will have, that will give you success. It is that which the Lord can do for you. We need to have far less confidence in what man can do, and far more confidence in what God can do for every believing soul. He longs to have you reach after Him by faith. He longs to have you expect great things from Him. He longs to give you understanding in temporal as well as in spiritual matters. He can sharpen the intellect. He can give tact and skill. Put your talents into the work, ask God for wisdom, and it will be given you.

Take the word of Christ as your assurance. Has He

[1] 1 Cor. 3:9

not invited you to come unto Him? Never allow yourself to talk in a hopeless, discouraged way. If you do, you will lose much. By looking at appearances, and complaining when difficulties and pressure come, you give evidence of a sickly, enfeebled faith. Talk and act as if your faith was invincible. The Lord is rich in resources; He owns the world. Look heavenward in faith. Look to Him who has light and power and efficiency.

There is in genuine faith a buoyancy, a steadfastness of principle, and a fixedness of purpose, that neither time nor toil can weaken. "Even the youths shall faint and be weary, and the young men shall utterly fall: but they that wait upon the Lord shall renew their strength; they shall mount up with wings as eagles; they shall run, and not be weary; and they shall walk, and not faint."[1]

There are many who long to help others, but they feel that they have no spiritual strength or light to impart. Let them present their petitions at the throne of grace. Plead for the Holy Spirit. God stands back of every promise He has made. With your Bible in your hands say, I have done as Thou hast said. I present Thy promise, "Ask, and it shall be given you; seek, and ye shall find; knock, and it shall be opened unto you."

We must not only pray in Christ's name, but by the inspiration of the Holy Spirit. This explains what is meant when it is said that the Spirit "maketh intercession for us, with groanings which can not be uttered."[2] Such prayer God delights to answer. When with earnestness and intensity we breathe a prayer in the name of Christ, there is in that very intensity a pledge from God that He is about to answer our prayer "exceeding abundantly above all that we ask or think."[3]

Christ has said, "What things soever ye desire, when ye

[1] Isa. 40:30, 31   [2] Rom. 8:26   [3] Eph. 3:20

pray, believe that ye receive them, and ye shall have them."
"Whatsoever ye shall ask in My name, that will I do, that
the Father may be glorified in the Son." And the beloved
John, under the inspiration of the Holy Spirit, speaks with
great plainness and assurance: "If we ask anything according
to His will, He heareth us: and if we know that He hear
us, whatsoever we ask, we know that we have the petitions
that we desired of Him."[1]   Then press your petition to the
Father in the name of Jesus. God will honor that name.

The rainbow round about the throne is an assurance
that God is true, that in Him is no variableness, neither
shadow of turning. We have sinned against Him, and are
undeserving of His favor; yet He Himself has put into our
lips that most wonderful of pleas, "Do not abhor us, for
Thy name's sake; do not disgrace the throne of Thy glory;
remember, break not Thy covenant with us."[2]   When we
come to Him confessing our unworthiness and sin, He has
pledged Himself to give heed to our cry. The honor of
His throne is staked for the fulfilment of His word unto us.

Like Aaron, who symbolized Christ, our Saviour bears
the names of all His people on His heart in the holy place.
Our great High Priest remembers all the words by which
He has encouraged us to trust. He is ever mindful of
His covenant.

All who seek of Him shall find. All who knock will
have the door opened to them. The excuse will not be
made, Trouble Me not; the door is closed; I do not wish
to open it. Never will one be told, I can not help you.
Those who beg at midnight for loaves to feed the hungry
souls will be successful.

In the parable, he who asks bread for the stranger
receives "as many as he needeth." And in what measure
will God impart to us that we may impart to others? —

[1] Mark 11:24; John 14:13; 1 John 5:14, 15   [2] Jer. 14 21

"According to the measure of the gift of Christ."[1]   Angels
are watching with intense interest to see how man is dealing
with his fellow-men.   When they see one manifest Christlike
sympathy for the erring, they press to his side, and bring to
his remembrance words to speak that will be as the bread
of life to the soul.   So "God shall supply all your need
according to His riches in glory by Christ Jesus."[2]   Your
testimony in its genuineness and reality He will make
powerful in the power of the life to come.   The word of
the Lord will be in your mouth as truth and righteousness.

Personal effort for others should be preceded by much
secret prayer; for it requires great wisdom to understand
the science of saving souls.   Before communicating with
men, commune with Christ.   At the throne of heavenly
grace obtain a preparation for ministering to the people.

Let your heart break for the longing it has for God, for
the living God.   The life of Christ has shown what humanity
can do by being partaker of the divine nature.   All that
Christ received from God we too may have.   Then ask
and receive.   With the persevering faith of Jacob, with the
unyielding persistence of Elijah, claim for yourself all that
God has promised.

Let the glorious conceptions of God possess your mind.
Let your life be knit by hidden links to the life of Jesus.
He who commanded the light to shine out of darkness is
willing to shine in your heart, to give the light of the
knowledge of the glory of God in the face of Jesus Christ.
The Holy Spirit will take the things of God and show
them unto you, conveying them as a living power into the
obedient heart.   Christ will lead you to the threshold of
the Infinite.   You may behold the glory beyond the veil,
and reveal to men the sufficiency of Him who ever liveth
to make intercession for us.

[1] Eph. 4 : 7   [2] Phil. 4 : 19

Two Worshipers

*U*NTO certain which trusted in themselves that they were righteous, and despised others," Christ spoke the parable of the Pharisee and the publican. The Pharisee goes up to the temple to worship, not because he feels that he is a sinner in need of pardon, but because he thinks himself righteous, and hopes to win commendation. His worship he regards as an act of merit that will recommend him to God. At the same time it will give the people a high opinion of his piety. He hopes to secure favor with both God and man. His worship is prompted by self-interest.

And he is full of self-praise. He looks it, he walks it, he prays it. Drawing apart from others as if to say, "Come not near to me; for I am holier than thou,"[1] he stands and prays "with himself." Wholly self-satisfied, he thinks that God and men regard him with the same complacency.

"God, I thank thee," he says, "that I am not as other men are, extortioners, unjust, adulterers, or even as this publican." He judges his character, not by the holy character of God, but by the character of other men. His mind is turned away from God to humanity. This is the secret of his self-satisfaction.

He proceeds to recount his good deeds: "I fast twice in the week, I give tithes of all that I possess." The religion of the Pharisee does not touch the soul. He is not seeking Godlikeness of character, a heart filled with love and mercy. He is satisfied with a religion that has to do only with the outward life. His righteousness is his own, — the fruit of his own works, and judged by a human standard.

Whoever trusts in himself that he is righteous, will despise others. As the Pharisee judges himself by other men, so he judges other men by himself. His righteousness is estimated by theirs, and the worse they are, the more righteous by contrast he appears. His self-righteousness leads to accusing. "Other men" he condemns as trans- gressors of God's law. Thus he is making manifest the very spirit of Satan, the accuser of the brethren. With this spirit it is impossible for him to enter into communion with God. He goes down to his house destitute of the divine blessing.

The publican had gone to the temple with other worshipers, but he soon drew apart from them, as unworthy to unite in their devotions. Standing afar off, he "would not lift up so much as his eyes unto heaven, but smote upon his breast," in bitter anguish and self-abhorrence. He felt that he had transgressed against God, that he was sinful and polluted. He could not expect even pity from those around him; for they looked upon him with contempt. He knew that he had no merit to commend him to God, and in utter self-despair he cried, "God be merciful to me, a sinner." He did not compare himself with others.

Overwhelmed with a sense of guilt, he stood as if alone in God's presence. His only desire was for pardon and peace, his only plea was the mercy of God. And he was blessed. "I tell you," Christ said, "this man went down to his house justified rather than the other."

The Pharisee and the publican represent two great classes into which those who come to worship God are divided. Their first two representatives are found in the first two children that were born into the world. Cain thought himself righteous, and he came to God with a thank-offering only. He made no confession of sin, and acknowledged no need of mercy. But Abel came with the blood that pointed to the Lamb of God. He came as a sinner, confessing himself lost; his only hope was the unmerited love of God. The Lord had respect to his offering, but to Cain and his offering He had not respect. The sense of need, the recognition of our poverty and sin, is the very first condition of acceptance with God. "Blessed are the poor in spirit; for theirs is the kingdom of heaven."[1]

For each of the classes represented by the Pharisee and the publican there is a lesson in the history of the apostle Peter. In his early discipleship Peter thought himself strong. Like the Pharisee, in his own estimation he was "not as other men are." When Christ on the eve of His betrayal forewarned His disciples, "All ye shall be offended because of Me this night," Peter confidently declared, "Although all shall be offended, yet will not I."[2] Peter did not know his own danger. Self-confidence misled him. He thought himself able to withstand temptation; but in a few short hours the test came, and with cursing and swearing he denied his Lord.

When the crowing of the cock reminded him of the words of Christ, surprised and shocked at what he had just

[1] Matt. 5 : 3   [2] Mark 14 : 27, 29

"He is full of self-praise. He looks it, he walks it, he prays it."

The publican " knew that he had no merit to commend him to God, and in utter self-despair he cried, 'God be merciful to me, a sinner.'"

done, he turned and looked at his Master.   At that moment
Christ looked at Peter, and beneath that grieved look, in
which compassion and love for him were blended, Peter
understood himself.   He went out and wept bitterly.   That
look of Christ's broke his heart.   Peter had come to the
turning-point, and ·bitterly did he repent his sin.   He was
like the publican in his contrition and repentance, and like
the publican he found mercy.   The look of Christ assured
him of pardon.

Now his self-confidence was gone.   Never again were
the old boastful assertions repeated.

Christ after His resurrection thrice tested Peter.   "Simon,
son of Jonas," He said, "lovest thou Me more than these?"
Peter did not now exalt himself above his brethren.   He
appealed to the One who could read his heart.   "Lord,"
he said, "Thou knowest all things; Thou knowest that I
love Thee."[1]

Then he received his commission.   A work broader and
more delicate than had heretofore been his was appointed
him.   Christ bade him feed the sheep and the lambs.   In
thus committing to his stewardship the souls for whom the
Saviour had laid down His own life, Christ gave to Peter
the strongest proof of confidence in his restoration.   The
once restless, boastful, self-confident disciple had become
subdued and contrite.   Henceforth he followed his Lord in
self-denial and self-sacrifice.   He was a partaker of Christ's
sufferings; and when Christ shall sit upon the throne of
His glory, Peter will be a partaker in His glory.

The evil that led to Peter's fall, and that shut out the
Pharisee from communion with God, is proving the ruin of
· thousands to-day.   There is nothing so offensive to God, or
so dangerous to the human soul, as pride and self-sufficiency.
Of all sins it is the most hopeless, the most incurable.

[1] John 21:15, 17

Peter's fall was not instantaneous, but gradual. Self-confidence led him to the belief that he was saved, and step after step was taken in the downward path, until he could deny his Master. Never can we safely put confidence in self, or feel, this side of heaven, that we are secure against temptation. Those who accept the Saviour, however sincere their conversion, should never be taught to say or to feel that they are saved. This is misleading. Every one should be taught to cherish hope and faith; but even when we give ourselves to Christ and know that He accepts us, we are not beyond the reach of temptation. God's word declares, "Many shall be purified, and made white, and tried."[1] Only he who endures the trial will receive the crown of life.[2]

Those who accept Christ, and in their first confidence say, I am saved, are in danger of trusting to themselves. They lose sight of their own weakness and their constant need of divine strength. They are unprepared for Satan's devices, and under temptation many, like Peter, fall into the very depths of sin. We are admonished, "Let him that thinketh he standeth, take heed lest he fall."[3] Our only safety is in constant distrust of self, and dependence on Christ.

It was necessary for Peter to learn his own defects of character, and his need of the power and grace of Christ. The Lord could not save him from trial, but He could have saved him from defeat. Had Peter been willing to receive Christ's warning, he would have been watching unto prayer. He would have walked with fear and trembling lest his feet should stumble. And he would have received divine help, so that Satan could not have gained the victory.

It was through self-sufficiency that Peter fell; and it was through repentance and humiliation that his feet were again established. In the record of his experience every repenting sinner may find encouragement. Though Peter

[1] Dan. 12:10   [2] James 1:12   [3] 1 Cor. 10:12

had grievously sinned, he was not forsaken. The words of Christ were written upon his soul, "I have prayed for thee, that thy faith fail not."[1]   In his bitter agony of remorse, this prayer, and the memory of Christ's look of love and pity, gave him hope.   Christ after His resurrection remembered Peter, and gave the angel the message for the women, "Go your way, tell His disciples and Peter that He goeth before you into Galilee; there shall ye see Him."[2]   Peter's repentance was accepted by the sin-pardoning Saviour.

And the same compassion that reached out to rescue Peter is extended to every soul who has fallen under temptation.   It is Satan's special device to lead man into sin, and then leave him, helpless and trembling, fearing to seek for pardon.   But why should we fear, when God has said, "Let him take hold of My strength, that he may make peace with Me; and he shall make peace with Me"?[3] Every provision has been made for our infirmities, every encouragement offered us to come to Christ.

Christ offered up His broken body to purchase back God's heritage, to give man another trial.   "Wherefore He is able also to save them to the uttermost that come unto God by Him, seeing He ever liveth to make intercession for them."[4]   By His spotless life, His obedience, His death on the cross of Calvary, Christ interceded for the lost race. And now, not as a mere petitioner does the Captain of our salvation intercede for us, but as a Conqueror claiming His victory.   His offering is complete, and as our Intercessor He executes His self-appointed work, holding before God the censer containing His own spotless merits and the prayers, confessions, and thanksgiving of His people.   Perfumed with the fragrance of His righteousness, these ascend to God as a sweet savor.   The offering is wholly acceptable, and pardon covers all transgression.

[1] Luke 22:32   [2] Mark 16:7   [3] Isa. 27:5   [4] Heb. 7:25

Christ has pledged Himself to be our substitute and surety, and He neglects no one. He who could not see human beings exposed to eternal ruin without pouring out His soul unto death in their behalf, will look with pity and compassion upon every soul who realizes that he can not save himself.

"*The crowing of the cock reminded him of the words of Christ.*"

He will look upon no trembling suppliant without raising him up. He who through His own atonement provided for man an infinite fund of moral power, will not fail to employ this power in our behalf. We may take our sins and sorrows to His feet; for He loves us. His every look and word invites our confidence. He will shape and mold our characters according to His own will.

In the whole Satanic force there is not power to overcome one soul who in simple trust casts himself on Christ. "He giveth power to the faint; and to them that have no might He increaseth strength."[1]

[1] Isa. 40 : 29

"If we confess our sins, He is faithful and just to forgive us our sins, and to cleanse us from all unrighteousness." The Lord says, "Only acknowledge thine iniquity, that thou hast transgressed against the Lord thy God." "Then will I sprinkle clean water upon you, and ye shall be clean; from all your filthiness and from all your idols will I cleanse you." [1]

But we must have a knowledge of ourselves, a knowledge that will result in contrition, before we can find pardon and peace. The Pharisee felt no conviction of sin. The Holy Spirit could not work with him. His soul was encased in a self-righteous armor which the arrows of God, barbed and true-aimed by angel hands, failed to penetrate. It is only he who knows himself to be a sinner that Christ can save. He came "to heal the broken-hearted, to preach deliverance to the captives, and recovering of sight to the blind, to set at liberty them that are bruised." [2] But "they that are whole need not a physician." [3] We must know our real condition, or we shall not feel our need of Christ's help. We must understand our danger, or we shall not flee to the refuge. We must feel the pain of our wounds, or we shall not desire healing.

The Lord says, "Because thou sayest, I am rich, and increased with goods, and have need of nothing; and knowest not that thou art wretched, and miserable, and poor, and blind, and naked: I counsel thee to buy of Me gold tried in the fire, that thou mayest be rich; and white raiment, that thou mayest be clothed, and that the shame of thy nakedness do not appear; and anoint thine eyes with eyesalve, that thou mayest see." [4] The gold tried in the fire is faith that works by love. Only this can bring us into harmony with God. We may be active, we may do much work; but without love, such love as dwelt in the heart of Christ, we can never be numbered with the family of heaven.

[1] 1 John 1 : 9; Jer. 3 : 13; Eze. 36 : 25   [2] Luke 4 : 18   [3] Luke 5 : 31   [4] Rev. 3 : 17, 18

No man can of himself understand his errors. "The heart is deceitful above all things, and desperately wicked; who can know it?"[1] The lips may express a poverty of soul that the heart does not acknowledge. While speaking to God of poverty of spirit, the heart may be swelling with the conceit of its own superior humility and exalted righteousness. In one way only can a true knowledge of self be obtained. We must behold Christ. It is ignorance of Him that makes men so uplifted in their own righteousness. When we contemplate His purity and excellence, we shall see our own weakness and poverty and defects as they really are. We shall see ourselves lost and hopeless, clad in garments of self-righteousness, like every other sinner. We shall see that if we are ever saved, it will not be through our own goodness, but through God's infinite grace.

The prayer of the publican was heard because it showed dependence reaching forth to lay hold upon Omnipotence. Self to the publican appeared nothing but shame. Thus it must be seen by all who seek God. By faith — faith that renounces all self-trust — the needy suppliant is to lay hold upon infinite power.

No outward observances can take the place of simple faith and entire renunciation of self. But no man can empty himself of self. We can only consent for Christ to accomplish the work. Then the language of the soul will be, Lord, take my heart; for I can not give it. It is Thy property. Keep it pure, for I can not keep it for Thee. Save me in spite of myself, my weak, unchristlike self. Mold me, fashion me, raise me into a pure and holy atmosphere, where the rich current of Thy love can flow through my soul.

It is not only at the beginning of the Christian life that this renunciation of self is to be made. At every advance step heavenward it is to be renewed. All our good works

[1] Jer. 17:9

are dependent on a power outside of ourselves. Therefore there needs to be a continual reaching out of the heart after God, a continual, earnest, heart-breaking confession of sin and humbling of the soul before Him. Only by constant renunciation of self and dependence on Christ can we walk safely.

The nearer we come to Jesus, and the more clearly we discern the purity of His character, the more clearly we shall discern the exceeding sinfulness of sin, and the less we shall feel like exalting ourselves. Those whom heaven recognizes as holy ones are the last to parade their own goodness. The apostle Peter became a faithful minister of Christ, and he was greatly honored with divine light and power; he had an active part in the upbuilding of Christ's church; but Peter never forgot the fearful experience of his humiliation; his sin was forgiven; yet well he knew that for the weakness of character which had caused his fall only the grace of Christ could avail. He found in himself nothing in which to glory.

None of the apostles or prophets ever claimed to be without sin. Men who have lived nearest to God, men who would sacrifice life itself rather than knowingly commit a wrong act, men whom God had honored with divine light and power, have confessed the sinfulness of their own nature. They have put no confidence in the flesh, have claimed no righteousness of their own, but have trusted wholly in the righteousness of Christ. So will it be with all who behold Christ.

At every advance step in Christian experience our repentance will deepen. It is to those whom the Lord has forgiven, to those whom He acknowledges as His people, that He says, "Then shall ye remember your own evil ways, and your doings that were not good, and shall loathe yourselves in your own sight."[1] Again He says, "I will establish My covenant with thee, and thou shalt know that I am the Lord; that thou mayest remember, and be confounded, and never open thy mouth any more because of thy shame, when I am pacified toward thee for all that thou hast done, saith the Lord God."[2] Then our lips will not be opened in self-glorification. We shall know that our sufficiency is in Christ alone. We shall make the apostle's confession our own, "I know that in me (that is, in my flesh) dwelleth no good thing." "God forbid that I should glory, save in the cross of our Lord Jesus Christ, by whom the world is crucified unto me, and I unto the world."[3]

In harmony with this experience is the command, "Work out your own salvation with fear and trembling. For it is God which worketh in you both to will and to do of His good pleasure."[4] God does not bid you fear that He will fail to fulfil His promises, that His patience will weary, or His compassion be found wanting. Fear lest your will shall not be held in subjection to Christ's will, lest your hereditary and cultivated traits of character shall control your life. "It is God which worketh in you both to will and to do of His good pleasure." Fear lest self shall interpose between your soul and the great Master-worker. Fear lest self-will shall mar the high purpose that, through you, God desires to accomplish. Fear to trust to your own strength, fear to withdraw your hand from the hand of Christ, and attempt to walk life's pathway without His abiding presence.

We need to shun everything that would encourage pride and self-sufficiency; therefore we should beware of giving or receiving flattery or praise. It is Satan's work to flatter. He deals in flattery as well as in accusing and condemnation. Thus he seeks to work the ruin of the soul. Those who

11   [1] Eze. 36 : 31   [2] Eze. 16 . 62, 63   [3] Rom. 7 : 18 ; Gal. 6 : 14   [4] Phil. 2 : 12, 13

give praise to men are used by Satan as his agents. Let the workers for Christ direct every word of praise away from themselves. Let self be put out of sight. Christ alone is to be exalted. "Unto Him that loved us, and washed us from our sins in His own blood,"[1] let every eye be directed, and praise from every heart ascend.

The life in which the fear of the Lord is cherished will not be a life of sadness and gloom. It is the absence of Christ that makes the countenance sad, and the life a pilgrimage of sighs. Those who are filled with self-esteem and self-love do not feel the need of a living, personal union with Christ. The heart that has not fallen on the Rock is proud of its wholeness. Men want a dignified religion. They desire to walk in a path wide enough to take in their own attributes. Their self-love, their love of popularity and love of praise, exclude the Saviour from their hearts, and without Him there is gloom and sadness. But Christ dwelling in the soul is a wellspring of joy. For all who receive Him, the very keynote of the word of God is rejoicing.

"For thus saith the high and lofty One that inhabiteth eternity, whose name is Holy: I dwell in the high and holy place, with Him also that is of a contrite and humble spirit, to revive the spirit of the humble, and to revive the heart of the contrite ones."[2]

It was when Moses was hidden in the cleft of the rock that he beheld the glory of God. It is when we hide in the riven Rock that Christ will cover us with His own pierced hand, and we shall hear what the Lord saith unto His servants. To us, as to Moses, God will reveal Himself as "merciful and gracious, long-suffering, and abundant in goodness and truth, keeping mercy for thousands, forgiving iniquity and transgression and sin."[3]

The work of redemption involves consequences of which

[1] Rev. 1:5   [2] Isa. 57:15   [3] Ex. 34:6, 7

it is difficult for man to have any conception. "Eye hath not seen, nor ear heard, neither have entered into the heart of man, the things which God hath prepared for them that love Him."[1] As the sinner, drawn by the power of Christ, approaches the uplifted cross, and prostrates himself before it, there is a new creation. A new heart is given him. He becomes a new creature in Christ Jesus. ˙Holiness finds that it has nothing more to require. God Himself is "the justifier of him which believeth in Jesus." And "whom He justified, them He also glorified."[2] Great as is the shame and degradation through sin, even greater will be the honor and exaltation through redeeming love. To human beings striving for conformity to the divine image there is imparted an outlay of heaven's treasure, an excellency of power, that will place them higher than even the angels who have never fallen.

"Thus saith the Lord, the Redeemer of Israel, and His Holy One, to him whom man despiseth, to him whom the nation abhorreth, . . . Kings shall see and arise, princes also shall worship, because of the Lord that is faithful, and the Holy One of Israel, and He shall choose thee."[3]

"For every one that exalteth himself shall be abased; and he that humbleth himself shall be exalted."

[1] 1 Cor. 2:9   [2] Rom. 3:26; 8:30   [3] Isa. 49:7

"Shall Not God Avenge His Own?"

*C*HRIST had been speaking of the period just before His second coming, and of the perils through which His followers must pass. With special reference to that time He related the parable "to this end, that men ought always to pray, and not to faint."

"There was in a city," He said, "a judge, which feared not God, neither regarded man; and there was a widow in that city; and she came unto him, saying, Avenge me of mine adversary. And he would not for a while; but afterward he said within himself, Though I fear not God, nor regard man; yet because this widow troubleth me, I will avenge her, lest by her continual coming she weary me. And the Lord said, Hear what the unjust judge saith. And shall not God avenge His own elect, which cry day and night unto Him, though He bear long with them? I tell you that He will avenge them speedily."

The judge who is here pictured had no regard for right,

Based on Luke 18. 1–8

nor pity for suffering. The widow who pressed her case before him was persistently repulsed. Again and again she came to him, only to be treated with contempt, and to be driven from the judgment-seat. The judge knew that her cause was righteous, and he could have relieved her at once, but he would not. He wanted to show his arbitrary power, and it gratified him to let her ask and plead and entreat in vain. But she would not fail nor become discouraged. Notwithstanding his indifference and hard-heartedness, she pressed her petition until the judge consented to attend to her case. "Though I fear not God, nor regard man," he said, "yet because this widow troubleth me, I will avenge her, lest by her continual coming she weary me." To save his reputation, to avoid giving publicity to his partial, one-sided judgment, he avenged the persevering woman.

"And the Lord said, Hear what the unjust judge saith. And shall not God avenge His own elect, which cry day and night unto Him, though He bear long with them? I tell you that He will avenge them speedily." Christ here draws a sharp contrast between the unjust judge and God. The judge yielded to the widow's request merely through selfishness, that he might be relieved of her importunity. He felt for her no pity or compassion; her misery was nothing to him. How different is the attitude of God toward those who seek Him. The appeals of the needy and distressed are considered by Him with infinite compassion.

The woman who entreated the judge for justice had lost her husband by death. Poor and friendless, she had no means of retrieving her ruined fortunes. So by sin, man lost his connection with God. Of himself he has no means of salvation. But in Christ we are brought nigh unto the Father. The elect of God are dear to His heart. They are those whom He has called out of darkness into His marvelous light, to show forth His praise, to shine as lights amid the darkness of the world. The unjust judge had no special interest in the widow who importuned him for deliverance; yet in order to rid himself of her pitiful appeals, he heard her plea, and delivered her from her adversary. But God loves His children with infinite love. To Him the dearest object on earth is His church.

"For the Lord's portion is His people; Jacob is the lot of His inheritance. He found him in a desert land, and in the waste, howling wilderness; He led him about, He instructed him, He kept him as the apple of His eye." "For thus saith the Lord of hosts: After the glory hath He sent me unto the nations which spoiled you; for he that toucheth you toucheth the apple of His eye."[1]

The widow's prayer, "Avenge me"—"do me justice"[2]—"of mine adversary," represents the prayer of God's children. Satan is their great adversary. He is the "accuser of our brethren," who accuses them before God day and night.[3] He is continually working to misrepresent and accuse, to deceive and destroy the people of God. And it is for deliverance from the power of Satan and his agents that in this parable Christ teaches His disciples to pray.

In the prophecy of Zechariah is brought to view Satan's accusing work, and the work of Christ in resisting the adversary of His people. The prophet says, "He showed me Joshua the high priest standing before the angel of the Lord, and Satan standing at his right hand to resist him. And the Lord said unto Satan, The Lord rebuke thee, O Satan; even the Lord that hath chosen Jerusalem rebuke thee: is not this a brand plucked out of the fire? Now Joshua was clothed with filthy garments, and stood before the angel."[4]

The people of God are here represented as a criminal

[1] Deut. 32:9, 10; Zech. 2:8   [2] R. V.   [3] Rev. 12:10   [4] Zech. 3:1-3

on trial.   Joshua, as high priest, is seeking for a blessing for his people, who are in great affliction.   While he is pleading before God, Satan is standing at his right hand as his adversary.   He is accusing the children of God, and making their case appear as desperate as possible.   He presents before the Lord their evil doings and their defects. He shows their faults and failures, hoping they will appear of such a character in the eyes of Christ that He will render them no help in their great need.   Joshua, as the representative of God's people, stands under condemnation, clothed with filthy garments.   Aware of the sins of his people, he is weighed down with discouragement. Satan is pressing upon his soul a sense of guiltiness that makes him feel almost hopeless.   Yet there he stands as a suppliant, with Satan arrayed against him.

The work of Satan as an accuser began in heaven.   This has been his work on earth ever since man's fall, and it will be his work in a special sense as we

"*And there was a widow in that city, and she came unto him, saying, Avenge me of mine adversary.*"

approach nearer to the close of this world's history.   As
he sees that his time is short, he will work with greater
earnestness to deceive and destroy.   He is angry when he
sees a people on the earth, who, even in their weakness
and sinfulness, have respect to the law of Jehovah.   He is
determined that they shall not obey God.   He delights in
their unworthiness, and has devices prepared for every soul,
that all may be ensnared and separated from God.   He
seeks to accuse and condemn God, and all who strive to
carry out His purposes in this world, in mercy and love,
in compassion and forgiveness.

Every manifestation of God's power for His people
arouses the enmity of Satan.   Every time God works in
their behalf, Satan with his angels works with renewed vigor
to compass their ruin.   He is jealous of all who make Christ
their strength.   His object is to instigate evil, and when he
has succeeded, throw all the blame upon the tempted ones.
He points to their filthy garments, their defective characters.
He presents their weakness and folly, their sins of ingrati-
tude, their unlikeness to Christ, which has dishonored their
Redeemer.   All this he urges as an argument proving his
right to work his will in their destruction.   He endeavors
to affright their souls with the thought that their case is
hopeless, that the stain of their defilement can never be
washed away.   He hopes so to destroy their faith that
they will yield fully to his temptations, and turn from their
allegiance to God.

The Lord's people can not of themselves answer the
charges of Satan.   As they look to themselves, they are
ready to despair.   But they appeal to the divine Advocate.
They plead the merits of the Redeemer.   God can be "just,
and the justifier of him which believeth in Jesus."[1]   With
confidence the Lord's children cry unto Him to silence the

[1] Rom. 3: 26

accusations of Satan, and bring to naught his devices. "Do me justice of mine adversary," they pray; and with the mighty argument of the cross, Christ silences the bold accuser.

"The Lord said unto Satan, The Lord rebuke thee, O Satan, even the Lord that hath chosen Jerusalem rebuke thee: is not this a brand plucked out of the fire?" When Satan seeks to cover the people of God with blackness, and ruin them, Christ interposes. Although they have sinned, Christ has taken the guilt of their sins upon His own soul. He has snatched the race as a brand from the fire. By His human nature He is linked with man, while through His divine nature He is one with the infinite God. Help is brought within the reach of perishing souls. The adversary is rebuked.

"Now Joshua was clothed with filthy garments, and stood before the angel: and he answered and spake unto those that stood before him, saying, Take away the filthy garments from him. And unto him he said, Behold, I have caused thine iniquity to pass from thee, and I will clothe thee with change of raiment. And I said, Let them set a fair miter upon his head. So they set a fair miter upon his head, and clothed him with garments." Then with the authority of the Lord of hosts the angel made a solemn pledge to Joshua, the representative of God's people: "If thou wilt walk in My ways, and if thou wilt keep My charge, then thou shalt also judge My house, and shalt also keep My courts, and I will give thee places to walk among these that stand by,"[1] — even among the angels that surround the throne of God.

Notwithstanding the defects of the people of God, Christ does not turn away from the objects of His care. He has the power to change their raiment. He removes the filthy

[1] Zech. 3 : 3-7

garments, He places upon the repenting, believing ones His own robe of righteousness, and writes pardon against their names on the records of heaven. He confesses them as His before the heavenly universe. Satan their adversary is shown to be an accuser and deceiver. God will do justice for His own elect.

The prayer, "Do me justice of mine adversary," applies not only to Satan, but to the agencies whom he instigates to misrepresent, to tempt, and to destroy the people of God. Those who have decided to obey the commandments of God will understand by experience that they have adversaries who are controlled by a power from beneath. Such adversaries beset Christ at every step, how constantly and determinedly no human being can ever know. Christ's disciples, like their Master, are followed by continual temptation.

The Scriptures describe the condition of the world just before Christ's second coming. James the apostle pictures the greed and oppression that will prevail. He says, "Go to now, ye rich men, . . . ye have heaped treasure together for the last days. Behold, the hire of the laborers who have reaped down your fields, which is of you kept back by fraud, crieth: and the cries of them which have reaped are entered into the ears of the Lord of Sabaoth. Ye have lived in pleasure on the earth, and been wanton. Ye have nourished your hearts, as in a day of slaughter. Ye have condemned and killed the just; and he doth not resist you."[1] This is a picture of what exists to-day. By every species of oppression and extortion, men are piling up colossal fortunes, while the cries of starving humanity are coming up before God.

"Judgment is turned away backward, and justice standeth afar off; for truth is fallen in the street, and equity can not

[1] James 5:1-6

enter. Yea, truth faileth; and he that departeth from evil maketh himself a prey."[1] This was fulfilled in the life of Christ on earth. He was loyal to God's commandments, setting aside the human traditions and requirements which had been exalted in their place. Because of this He was hated and persecuted. This history is repeated. The laws and traditions of men are exalted above the law of God, and those who are true to God's commandments suffer reproach and persecution. Christ, because of His faithfulness to God, was accused as a Sabbath-breaker and blasphemer. He was declared to be possessed of a devil, and was denounced as Beelzebub. In like manner His followers are accused and misrepresented. Thus Satan hopes to lead them to sin, and cast dishonor upon God.

The character of the judge in the parable, who feared not God nor regarded man, was presented by Christ to show the kind of judgment that was then being executed, and that would soon be witnessed at His trial. He desires His people in all time to realize how little dependence can be placed on earthly rulers or judges in the day of adversity. Often the elect people of God have to stand before men in official positions, who do not make the word of God their guide and counselor, but who follow their own unconsecrated, undisciplined impulses.

In the parable of the unjust judge, Christ has shown what we should do. "Shall not God avenge His own elect, which cry day and night unto Him?" Christ, our example, did nothing to vindicate or deliver Himself. He committed His case to God. So His followers are not to accuse or condemn, or to resort to force in order to deliver themselves.

When trials arise that seem unexplainable, we should not allow our peace to be spoiled. However unjustly we may be treated, let not passion arise. By indulging a spirit

[1] Isa. 59:14, 15

of retaliation we injure ourselves. We destroy our own confidence in God, and grieve the Holy Spirit. There is by our side a witness, a heavenly messenger, who will lift up for us a standard against the enemy. He will shut us in with the bright beams of the Sun of Righteousness. Beyond this Satan can not penetrate. He can not pass this shield of holy light.

While the world is progressing in wickedness, none of us need flatter ourselves that we shall have no difficulties. But it is these very difficulties that bring us into the audience-chamber of the Most High. We may seek counsel of One who is infinite in wisdom.

The Lord says, "Call upon Me in the day of trouble."[1] He invites us to present to Him our perplexities and necessities, and our need of divine help. He bids us be instant in prayer. As soon as difficulties arise, we are to offer to Him our sincere, earnest petitions. By our importunate prayers we give evidence of our strong confidence in God. The sense of our need leads us to pray earnestly, and our Heavenly Father is moved by our supplications.

Often those who suffer reproach or persecution for their faith are tempted to think themselves forsaken by God. In the eyes of men they are in the minority. To all appearance their enemies triumph over them. But let them not violate their conscience. He who has suffered in their behalf, and has borne their sorrows and afflictions, has not forsaken them.

The children of God are not left alone and defenseless. Prayer moves the arm of Omnipotence. Prayer has "subdued kingdoms, wrought righteousness, obtained promises, stopped the mouths of lions, quenched the violence of fire"— we shall know what this means when we hear the reports of the martyrs who died for their faith,—"turned to flight the armies of the aliens."[2]

[1] Ps. 50:15   [2] Heb. 11:33, 34

If we surrender our lives to His service, we can never be placed in a position for which God has not made provision. Whatever may be our situation, we have a Guide to direct our way; whatever our perplexities, we have a sure Counselor;

"Go to now, ye rich men, . . . ye have heaped treasure together for the last days."

whatever our sorrow, bereavement, or loneliness, we have a sympathizing Friend. If in our ignorance we make missteps, Christ does not leave us. His voice, clear and distinct, is heard saying, "I am the Way, the Truth, and the Life."[1] "He shall deliver the needy when he crieth; the poor also, and him that hath no helper."[2]

The Lord declares that He will be honored by those who draw nigh to Him, who faithfully do His service. "Thou

[1]John 14:6   [2]Ps. 72:12

wilt keep him in perfect peace whose mind is stayed on Thee, because he trusteth in Thee."[1]   The arm of Omnipotence is outstretched to lead us onward and still onward. Go forward, the Lord says; I will send you help. It is for My name's glory that you ask, and you shall receive. I will be honored before those who are watching for your failure. They shall see My word triumph gloriously. "All things whatsoever ye shall ask in prayer, believing, ye shall receive."[2]

Let all who are afflicted or unjustly used, cry to God. Turn away from those whose hearts are as steel, and make your requests known to your Maker. Never is one repulsed who comes to Him with a contrite heart. Not one sincere prayer is lost. Amid the anthems of the celestial choir, God hears the cries of the weakest human being. We pour out our heart's desire in our closets, we breathe a prayer as we walk by the way, and our words reach the throne of the Monarch of the universe. They may be inaudible to any human ear, but they can not die away into silence, nor can they be lost through the activities of business that are going on. Nothing can drown the soul's desire. It rises above the din of the street, above the confusion of the multitude to the heavenly courts. It is God to whom we are speaking and our prayer is heard.

You who feel the most unworthy, fear not to commit your case to God. When He gave Himself in Christ for the sin of the world, He undertook the case of every soul "He that spared not His own Son, but delivered Him up for us all, how shall He not with Him also freely give us all things?"[3] Will He not fulfil the gracious word given for our encouragement and strength?

Christ desires nothing so much as to redeem His heritage from the dominion of Satan. But before we are delivered from Satan's power without, we must be delivered from his

[1] Isa 26:3   [2] Matt. 21:22   [3] Rom. 8:32

power within. The Lord permits trials in order that we may be cleansed from earthliness, from selfishness, from harsh, unchristlike traits of character. He suffers the deep waters of affliction to go over our souls, in order that we may know Him, and Jesus Christ whom He has sent, in order that we may have deep heart-longings to be cleansed from defilement, and may come forth from the trial purer, holier, happier. Often we enter the furnace of trial with our souls darkened with selfishness; but if patient under the crucial test, we shall come forth reflecting the divine character. When His purpose in the affliction is accomplished, "He shall bring forth thy righteousness as the light, and thy judgment as the noonday."[1]

There is no danger that the Lord will neglect the prayers of His people. The danger is that in temptation and trial they will become discouraged, and fail to persevere in prayer.

The Saviour manifested divine compassion toward the Syrophenician woman. His heart was touched as He saw her grief. He longed to give her an immediate assurance that her prayer was heard; but He desired to teach His disciples a lesson, and for a time He seemed to neglect the cry of her tortured heart. When her faith had been made manifest, He spoke to her words of commendation, and sent her away with the precious boon she had asked. The disciples never forgot this lesson, and it is placed on record to show the result of persevering prayer.

It was Christ Himself who put into that mother's heart the persistence which would not be repulsed. It was Christ who gave the pleading widow courage and determination before the judge. It was Christ who, centuries before, in the mysterious conflict by the Jabbok, had inspired Jacob with the same persevering faith. And the confidence which He Himself had implanted, He did not fail to reward.

[1] Ps. 37 : 6

He who dwells in the heavenly sanctuary judges righteously. His pleasure is more in His people, struggling with temptation in a world of sin, than in the host of angels that surround His throne.

In this speck of a world the whole heavenly universe manifests the greatest interest; for Christ has paid an infinite price for the souls of its inhabitants. The world's Redeemer has bound earth to heaven by ties of intelligence; for the redeemed of the Lord are here. Heavenly beings still visit the earth, as in the days when they walked and talked with Abraham and with Moses. Amid the busy activity of our great cities, amid the multitudes that crowd the thoroughfares and fill the marts of trade, where from morning till evening the people act as if business and sport and pleasure were all there is to life, where there are so few to contemplate unseen realities, — even here heaven has still its watchers and its holy ones. There are invisible agencies observing every word and deed of human beings. In every assembly for business or pleasure, in every gathering for worship, there are more listeners than can be seen with the natural sight. Sometimes the heavenly intelligences draw aside the curtain which hides the unseen world, that our thoughts may be withdrawn from the hurry and rush of life, to consider that there are unseen witnesses to all we do or say.

We need to understand better than we do the mission of the angel visitants. It would be well to consider that in all our work we have the co-operation and care of heavenly beings. Invisible armies of light and power attend the meek and lowly ones who believe and claim the promises of God. Cherubim and seraphim and angels that excel in strength,— ten thousand times ten thousand and thousands of thousands, —stand at His right hand, "all ministering spirits, sent forth to minister for them who shall be heirs of salvation."[1]

[1] Heb. 1 : 14

By these angel messengers a faithful record is kept of the words and deeds of the children of men. Every act of cruelty or injustice toward God's people, all they are caused to suffer through the power of evil workers, is registered in heaven.

"Shall not God avenge His own elect, which cry day and night unto Him, though He bear long with them? I tell you that He will avenge them speedily."

"Cast not away therefore your confidence, which hath great recompense of reward. For ye have need of patience, that, after ye have done the will of God, ye might receive the promise. For yet a little while, and He that shall come will come, and will not tarry."[1] "Behold, the husbandman waiteth for the precious fruit of the earth, and hath long patience for it, until he receive the early and latter rain. Be ye also patient; stablish your hearts; for the coming of the Lord draweth nigh."[2]

The long-suffering of God is wonderful. Long does justice wait while mercy pleads with the sinner. But "righteousness and judgment are the establishment of His throne."[3] "The Lord is slow to anger;" but He is "great in power, and will not at all acquit the wicked: the Lord hath His way in the whirlwind and in the storm, and the clouds are the dust of His feet."[4]

The world has become bold in transgression of God's law. Because of His long forbearance, men have trampled upon His authority. They have strengthened one another in oppression and cruelty toward His heritage, saying, "How doth God know? and is there knowledge in the Most High?"[5] But there is a line beyond which they can not pass. The time is near when they will have reached the prescribed limit. Even now they have almost exceeded the bounds of the long-suffering of God, the limits of His

12   [1] Heb. 10 : 35-37   [2] James 5 . 7, 8   [3] Ps. 97 : 2, margin   [4] Nahum 1 : 3   [5] Ps. 73 : 11

grace, the limits of His mercy. The Lord will interpose to vindicate His own honor, to deliver His people, and to repress the swellings of unrighteousness.

In Noah's day, men had disregarded the law of God, until almost all remembrance of the Creator had passed away from the earth. Their iniquity reached so great a height that the Lord brought a flood of waters upon the earth, and swept away its wicked inhabitants.

From age to age the Lord has made known the manner of His working. When a crisis has come, He has revealed Himself, and has interposed to hinder the working out of Satan's plans. With nations, with families, and with individuals, He has often permitted matters to come to a crisis, that His interference might become marked. Then He has made manifest that there is a God in Israel who will maintain His law and vindicate His people.

In this time of prevailing iniquity we may know that the last great crisis is at hand. When the defiance of God's law is almost universal, when His people are oppressed and afflicted by their fellow-men, the Lord will interpose.

The time is near when He will say, "Come, My people enter thou into thy chambers, and shut thy doors about thee: hide thyself as it were for a little moment, until the indignation be overpast. For, behold, the Lord cometh out of His place to punish the inhabitants of the earth for their iniquity; the earth also shall disclose her blood, and shall no more cover her slain."[1] Men who claim to be Christians may now defraud and oppress the poor; they may rob the widow and the fatherless; they may indulge their Satanic hatred because they can not control the consciences of God's people; but for all this God will bring them into judgment. They "shall have judgment without mercy" that have "showed no mercy."[2] Not long hence they will stand before

[1] Isa. 26: 20, 21   [2] James 2: 13

the Judge of all the earth, to render an account for the pain they have caused to the bodies and souls of His heritage. They may now indulge in false accusations, they may deride those whom God has appointed to do His work, they may consign His believing ones to prison, to the chain-gang, to banishment, to death; but for every pang of anguish, every tear shed, they must answer. God will reward them double for their sins. Concerning Babylon, the symbol of the apostate church, He says to His ministers of judgment, "Her sins have reached unto heaven, and God hath remembered her iniquities. Reward her even as she rewarded you, and double unto her double according to her works: in the cup which she hath filled fill to her double."[1]

From India, from Africa, from China, from the islands of the sea, from the down-trodden millions of so-called Christian lands, the cry of human woe is ascending to God. That cry will not long be unanswered. God will cleanse the earth from its moral corruption, not by a sea of water as in Noah's day, but by a sea of fire that can not be quenched by any human devising.

"There shall be a time of trouble, such as never was since there was a nation even to that same time; and at that time Thy people shall be delivered every one that shall be found written in the book."[2]

From garrets, from hovels, from dungeons, from scaffolds, from mountains and deserts, from the caves of the earth and the caverns of the sea, Christ will gather His children to Himself. On earth they have been destitute, afflicted, and tormented. Millions have gone down to the grave loaded with infamy because they refused to yield to the deceptive claims of Satan. By human tribunals the children of God have been adjudged the vilest of criminals. But the day is near when "God is judge Himself."[3] Then the decisions

[1] Rev. 18 : 5, 6   [2] Dan. 12 : 1   [3] Ps. 50 : 6

of earth shall be reversed. "The rebuke of His people shall He take away." White robes will be given to every one of them. And "they shall call them the holy people, the redeemed of the Lord."[1]

Whatever crosses they have been called to bear, whatever losses they have sustained, whatever persecution they have suffered, even to the loss of their temporal life, the children of God are amply recompensed. "They shall see His face; and His name shall be in their foreheads."[2]

[1] Isa. 25:8; Rev. 6:11; Isa. 62.12　　　[2] Rev. 22:.

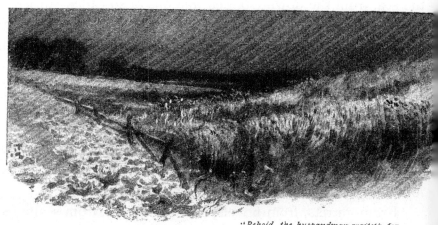

"*Behold, the husbandman waiteth for the precious fruit of the earth, and hath long patience for it, until he receive the early and latter rain.*"

This is the end of this publication.

Any remaining blank pages are for our book binding requirements and are blank on purpose.

To search thousands of interesting publications like this one, please remember to visit our website at:

http://www.kessinger.net

CPSIA information can be obtained at www.ICGtesting.com
Printed in the USA
LVOW04s0536061214

417402LV00003B/238/P